A BUSINESS APPROACH TO PETUNIA FARMING

Complete Entrepreneurial Step By Step Guide To Petunia Garden From Scratch

ZHURI HART

DISCLAIMER

This book is intended to provide general information and insights on adopting a business approach to farming. The content within is based on the author's knowledge and experiences up to the date of publication. It is essential to recognize that the field of agriculture is dynamic, influenced by various factors such as market conditions, climate, and regulatory changes.

Readers are advised to conduct thorough research, seek professional advice, and consider their unique circumstances before implementing any strategies or practices discussed in this book. The author and publisher disclaim any responsibility for the accuracy, completeness, or suitability of the information provided. The book is not a substitute for professional advice, and the author and publisher shall not be liable for any damages or losses arising from the use or reliance on the information presented herein.

Individual results may vary, and success in farming enterprises is contingent upon numerous variables. The author encourages readers to consult with relevant experts, agricultural extension services, and legal or financial professionals to tailor strategies to their specific needs and local conditions.

This book is not intended to be a comprehensive guide to all aspects of farming, and readers should exercise their judgment and discretion in applying the principles discussed. The author and publisher do not endorse any specific products, services, or companies mentioned in this book unless explicitly stated.

By reading this book, the reader acknowledges and accepts the inherent uncertainties in agricultural endeavors and agrees to use the information at their own risk.

TABLE OF CONTENTS

ABOUT THE BOOK

The thorough manual "A Business Approach to Petunia Farming" aims to provide readers with a strategic grasp of the petunia farming sector. The book starts with a thorough Introduction that explores the history of petunia farming and highlights its importance in the field of agriculture. The book's goals are established, laying the groundwork for an organized and educational investigation.

Understanding Petunias provides a summary of botany, introduces different kinds, and describes ideal growing conditions. For readers to make wise decisions throughout their petunia gardening experience, this fundamental knowledge is essential. After that, the part on market analysis offers a comprehensive analysis of customer demand, market trends, and competitor analysis. These insights are crucial for developing business strategies that work.

The parts on business planning and crop management comprise the bulk of the book. The book walks readers through the steps of starting a petunia farm, looking into several business models, and carrying out a thorough risk analysis. In-depth details on planting, fertilizer, pest management, and soil preparation guarantee that readers have the resources they need for productive farming.

Another important topic in the book is greenhouse techniques, which emphasize the benefits of petunia cultivation in a controlled environment. Precise attention is paid to harvesting and post-harvest handling, emphasizing the best possible timing, quality assurance, and efficient packaging to optimize market value.

An essential part on marketing strategies, which provides advice on positioning, branding, and building strong connections with merchants. Additionally, financial management is covered, with a focus on budgeting; income forecasts, and cost estimation, to help readers successfully traverse the financial terrain of petunia farming.

Legal considerations gives readers a better grasp of the laws, licenses, permissions, and intellectual property rights about petunia cultivation. A futuristic section on Future Trends in Petunia Farming, which explores cutting-edge technologies, eco-friendly methods, and inventions that will influence the sector going ahead, wraps out the book.

"A Business Approach to Petunia Farming" is an invaluable tool for professionals in the field as well as aspiring growers of petunias, providing a comprehensive overview that addresses everything from growing methods to marketing plans, regulatory issues, and emerging trends.

CHAPTER ONE

PETUNIA FARMING INTRODUCTION

OVERVIEW

Petunia cultivation has become a prominent horticultural technique in the field of agriculture, adding to the colorful tapestry of the floral sector. The origins of petunia farming can be found in South America, the original home of these vibrant and adaptable flowers. Petunias are grown in many parts of the world because of their fascinating blooms and capacity to withstand a variety of conditions, which has made them extremely popular over time.

The history of petunia cultivation dates back to the 19th century when these vivid flowers were initially brought to the continent by European horticulturists and botanists. The transition of petunias from wildflowers to domesticated decorative plants started with their voyage from South America to Europe. Since then, numerous Petunia variants have been created by meticulous breeding and hybridization, each with distinctive colors, patterns, and traits. The current state of petunia farming is largely the result of this evolutionary process.

RELEVANCE OF GROWING PETUNIAS

Beyond its historical foundation, petunia cultivation is significant for several reasons that make it a useful practice in the agricultural field. The economic value attached to growing petunias is one of the main factors contributing to the significance of this industry. With their vivid colors and varied designs, petunias have established themselves as industry mainstays in the floriculture sector. Growers now enjoy a profitable market thanks to the growing demand for petunias in gardening, landscaping, and flower arrangements, which supports the agricultural industry's economic viability.

Moreover, because they are so simple to grow and care for, petunias are incredibly popular among gardeners and horticulturists. These flowers are renowned for their hardiness, capacity to adjust to various soil types, and relative resistance to illnesses and pests. This opens up petunia gardening to a diverse group of fans, from seasoned pros to novice gardeners. The democratization of floral beauty is facilitated by the inclusion of Petunia cultivation, which makes it possible for people with different skill levels to appreciate and grow these lovely flowers.

Beyond the financial and practical benefits, petunia gardening is essential for improving the visual appeal of rural and urban environments. Petunias are a popular choice for enhancing public areas, parks, and home gardens because of their vivid colors and patterns. These flowers' aesthetic value enhances not only the surrounding area but also the general well-being of communities by encouraging a relationship with nature.

The history and significance of petunia cultivation are deeply entwined with the fields of floriculture and horticulture. From their wildflower beginnings in South America to their widespread cultivation around the world, petunias have evolved into beloved decorative plants. Petunia farming's economic worth, accessibility, and aesthetic qualities all work together to highlight its importance within the larger agricultural scene.

CHAPTER TWO

RECOGNIZING PETUNIAS

As members of the Solanaceae family, petunias are colorful and widely-used blooming plants that are prized for their ornamental appeal and range of colors. In terms of botany, they belong to the genus Petunia, which includes several species as well as several hybrids and cultivars. Originating in South America, specifically Argentina and Uruguay, these annuals are now grown all over the world for their eye-catching flowers.

OVERVIEW OF BOTANY

Caterpillar plants, or petunias, are distinguished by their funnel-shaped, frequently aromatic blossoms. Their growth style is usually spreading or trailing, which makes them ideal for borders, hanging baskets, and containers. Petunia leaves are typically oval and have a slightly sticky texture. The trumpet-shaped flowers of petunias, which vary in size depending on the cultivar, are one of their distinguishing characteristics. Petunia blooms come in a wide variety of colors, such as pink, purple, red, white, and bicolor combinations.

PETUNIA VARIETIES

The wide range of petunias found in the horticulture market can be roughly divided into three categories: grandiflora, multiflora, and milliflora. Large, eye-catching flowers are the hallmark of grandiflora petunias, which are frequently utilized as focal points in landscape designs. However, multiflora petunias yield an abundance of blooms in exchange for smaller blossoms, which makes them ideal for bulk planting. Multiflora petunias are perfect for ground cover or edging because of their small stature and profusion of tiny flowers.

In addition to these broad classifications, innumerable hybrids and cultivars have been created to meet particular needs and growing circumstances.

While some petunias have a more compact and bushy growth type, others may be bred for their trailing or mounding behaviors. Breeders have also concentrated on improving characteristics like disease resistance, color intensity, and blossom size, giving gardeners a plethora of options.

GROWING CONDITIONS

Petunias need well-drained soil that has a pH between slightly acidic and neutral. They also need enough sunlight to grow and bloom, and they work best in full sun for at least six hours each day. Though they can survive a variety of soil types, these plants are well suited to a loamy, fertile foundation. Watering petunias regularly is crucial, but be careful not to let them get too wet—too wet circumstances can lead to root rot.

Petunias are typically thought of as annuals, however in warmer areas, several varieties have perennial qualities. Frequent deadheading, or the removal of spent flowers, promotes ongoing flowering and keeps the area looking neat. Strong growth and profuse flowering can be further encouraged by fertilizing with a balanced, water-soluble fertilizer. Petunias are popular among both novice and experienced gardeners due to their versatility as attractive plants that can bring a pop of color and texture to gardens, balconies, and hanging baskets.

CHAPTER THREE

EXAMINATION OF THE MARKET

CURRENT PETUNIA MARKET TRENDS

There have been significant changes in consumer preferences and industry dynamics in the petunia market in recent years. The growing need for environmentally safe and sustainable petunia products is one such trend.

Customers are increasingly looking for petunias that are cultivated and grown using environmentally friendly methods as they become more concerned about environmental issues. Numerous industry participants have embraced eco-friendly packaging and sustainable farming practices as a result of this trend, which reflects a larger movement towards ecologically conscious decisions.

The emergence of Internet sales channels is a noteworthy development in the petunia industry.

The ease of use and accessibility provided by e-commerce platforms have changed the way petunia purchases are made by customers. Petunia businesses are adjusting their marketing tactics to develop a strong online presence as internet retail continues to gain pace. In addition to giving customers more options, this trend puts traditional brick-and-mortar stores under pressure to improve the customer experience to stay competitive.

CUSTOMER INQUIRY

A key factor influencing the dynamics of the petunia market is consumer demand. Demand for specialty and high-end petunia types are rising in the market. Unique and unusual species can command a premium price from petunia lovers, therefore suppliers and breeders must concentrate on expanding their product lines to meet this specialized market. Furthermore, petunias with particular qualities—like low maintenance, vivid colors, and unique scents—are becoming more and more popular.

Consumers are also looking for information and transparency on the petunia farming and sourcing processes. The industry has changed to provide comprehensive product information, such as the petunia's origin, production techniques, and any environmental or social certifications, in response to consumer desire for transparency. Petunia firms are realizing the value of clear communication in fostering trust as consumers become more scrutinized about the things they buy.

ANALYSIS OF COMPETITORS

There is fierce competition in the petunia business amongst growers, distributors, and breeders, among other stakeholders. For companies to comprehend the advantages and disadvantages of their competitors and spot areas where they may stand out, competitor analysis is essential. To gain a competitive edge in terms of color variations, disease resistance, and climate adaptation, breeders are always coming up with new and improved petunia varieties.

Growers and distributors are important participants in the competitive environment in addition to breeders. To satisfy customer demand and stay competitive in the market, effective supply chain management and distribution networks are essential.

Businesses are putting money into cutting-edge technologies to optimize their production workflows, cut expenses, and raise the general standard of their petunias.

Furthermore, the use of marketing methods is essential in differentiating one petunia brand from another. To establish a strong market presence, businesses are utilizing branding, social media, and digital marketing.

Companies trying to establish a long-term presence in the Petunia market frequently concentrate on cultivating a loyal client base through marketing initiatives, customer interaction, and post-purchase support.

The fierce competition among industry participants and changing consumer tastes are what drive the dynamic nature of the petunia business. To succeed in this booming industry, firms need to stay aware of the latest trends, comprehend customer needs, and perform thorough research on their competitors.

CHAPTER FOUR

PLANNING A BUSINESS

PUTTING UP A FARM FOR PETUNIAS

To ensure a profitable endeavor, starting a petunia farm involves careful consideration of several things. The first step is to choose a spot that will best support petunia growth, with ideal soil conditions, sunlight exposure, and climate. To ensure steady moisture levels, adequate irrigation systems and water supplies should be set up. Furthermore, infrastructure such as shade structures or greenhouses could be necessary to shield the petunias from pests and harsh weather.

BUSINESS PLANS FOR GROWING PETUNIAS

Business models are essential to the profitability of petunia farming operations. Several variables, including market demand, operational scale, and resource availability, influence the choice of business model. Petunias are sold directly to consumers through farmer's markets, internet retailers, or in-store retail under a direct-to-consumer business model. A wholesale approach, on the other hand, concentrates on providing petunias to merchants, nurseries, and landscaping businesses. To diversify revenue streams, some petunia farms might also use a hybrid business strategy that incorporates both direct-to-consumer and wholesale strategies.

EVALUATION AND CONTROL OF RISKS

Any business plan for petunia cultivation must include risk assessment and management. The venture's success may be impacted by several concerns, including operational problems, pest infestations, weather-related difficulties, and market volatility. Farmers can identify possible dangers and create effective mitigation or management measures by carrying out a thorough risk analysis. Investing in pest control techniques, diversifying product offerings, and putting in place appropriate insurance coverage are a few examples of risk management tactics that can help protect the petunia farm from unforeseen difficulties.

Financial factors are critical in the field of risk assessment. Petunia farming entrepreneurs need to carefully anticipate their budget, accounting for possible revenue streams, ongoing operating expenses, and setup fees. Understanding customer preferences, demand patterns, and pricing dynamics all depend on market research. Farmers can decide on resource allocation, pricing strategies, and sustainable growth by doing a thorough financial analysis.

Petunia growers should also create backup plans in case something unforeseen happens that affects their business. This entails setting up emergency response plans for natural disasters, having backup sources for crucial inputs, and keeping a flexible staff that can adjust to demand swings. In addition to reducing the effect of possible difficulties, a strong risk management strategy sets up the petunia farm for long-term resilience and success in the cutthroat industry.

Starting a petunia farm requires meticulous planning, strategic decision-making, and a deep comprehension of the dangers that are specific to agriculture. Petunia farmers should position their farms for sustained growth and profitability in the ever-changing floral sector by implementing effective risk management strategies, adopting appropriate business models, and carrying out thorough risk assessments.

CHAPTER FIVE

MANAGEMENT OF CROPS

FERTILIZATION AND SOIL PREPARATION

The foundation of good crop management is healthy soil and fertilization, which are necessary for maximum plant growth and output. To prepare the soil for planting, several techniques are used, including harrowing, cultivating, and plowing. These practices aid in increasing water infiltration, aeration, and breaking up soil compaction. Furthermore, adding organic matter to the soil improves its general fertility and nutrient availability.

To provide plants with the nutrients they need to flourish, fertilization is a crucial part of crop management. It's critical to comprehend the nutrient needs of particular crops, and farmers frequently test their soil to determine nutrient levels. Fertilizers are used to augment nutrients that are lacking based on these findings.

To avoid nutrient imbalances, which can have a detrimental effect on crop health and output, balanced fertilization is essential. For long-term soil health, sustainable methods like planting cover crops and applying organic fertilizers are becoming more and more important.

PLANTING & BRINGING IN PLANTS

A crucial part of crop management is planting and transplanting, which affects the crop's establishment and success. When planting, seed choice, spacing, and depth are important factors to take into account. Arranging seeds correctly guarantees consistent growth and promotes efficient use of available resources. To optimize the growing season, planting time must take into account seasonal fluctuations and climatic circumstances.

Transferring seedlings from nurseries to the field is known as transplanting, and it helps establish robust, healthy plants. This procedure guarantees a more uniform crop stand and gives you more control over plant spacing. Avoiding transplant shock and encouraging healthy establishment in the field require adequate care while transplanting, which includes avoiding root disturbance and providing suitable irrigation.

IRRIGATING AND WATERING

Crop success is largely dependent on effective water management and effective irrigation and watering techniques are critical elements of crop management. Sufficient moisture levels in the soil are essential for plant germination, growth, and the development of reproductive systems.

Climate conditions, crop water requirements, and soil type are some of the variables that affect how often and how much water is applied.

Based on crop needs and resource availability, irrigation systems are used, ranging from conventional approaches like furrow and flood irrigation to more contemporary ones like drip and sprinkler systems.

Farmers may increase total water-use efficiency, eliminate waste, and optimize water use with precision irrigation systems. In addition to promoting crop growth, strategic water management protects water supplies and lessens the negative effects of water scarcity on agriculture.

CONTROL OF PESTS AND DISEASES

One of crop management's ongoing challenges is safeguarding crops from pests and illnesses. Biological, chemical, and cultural control techniques are all combined in integrated pest management (IPM) approaches to effectively manage pest populations. Using resistant cultivars, rotating crops, and companion planting are a few cultural techniques that might lessen insect impact.

To reduce pest populations biologically, natural enemies like parasites and predators are introduced. Although chemical control is a widely used technique, it is used carefully to reduce its negative effects on the environment and prevent the emergence of pesticide resistance. To carry out prompt actions, monitoring and early detection of pest and disease outbreaks are essential. Resilient ecosystems are less dependent on chemical inputs because they can better survive the stresses of disease and pests. This is made possible by the adoption of sustainable practices and the promotion of biodiversity.

CHAPTER SIX

GREENHOUSE TECHNIQUES

BENEFITS OF AGRICULTURE IN GREENHOUSES

Growing a wide variety of crops in greenhouses is becoming more and more popular due to its many benefits. Controlling and optimizing environmental conditions is one important benefit. The perfect growing environment for plants may be created in greenhouses by carefully controlling the temperature, humidity, and light levels. This control increases crop productivity overall while also lengthening the growing season.

Moreover, crops that would be difficult to produce in open fields due to certain temperature requirements can be cultivated in greenhouses thanks to their regulated environment. Because of their versatility, farmers can experiment with growing high-value or exotic crops, which may be less able to adapt to changing environmental conditions.

The effects of unfavorable weather, such as strong winds, heavy rain, or extremely high temperatures, are also lessened by greenhouse farming. In addition to lowering crop losses, this protection against erratic weather patterns guarantees a more steady and consistent yield. Furthermore, the regulated setting reduces the likelihood of pests and illnesses, resulting in crops that are healthier and produce more.

HOW TO BUILD AND FURNISH A GREENHOUSE

For a greenhouse to be practical and efficient, many elements must be carefully considered while designing and putting it up. The plan, materials, and structure of the greenhouse should be chosen with the particular requirements of the crops that will be grown in mind. To maximize plant growth, elements including irrigation systems, ventilation, and sunshine exposure must be carefully managed.

Additionally, eco-friendly materials, water-saving techniques, and energy-efficient heating and cooling systems should all be incorporated into the design of the greenhouse. The integration of contemporary technology, such as automatic climate control and monitoring systems, can improve operating efficiency and save resource usage.

PETUNIA CONTROLLED ENVIRONMENT AGRICULTURE

Within greenhouse farming, controlled environment agriculture (CEA) is a specialized technique whose use for crops such as petunias demonstrates its accuracy and versatility. Temperature, humidity, light, and nutrient levels are just a few of the environmental variables that are carefully regulated in CEA to provide the ideal conditions for particular crops.

Because petunias are susceptible to changes in their environment, CEA makes sure that they grow in optimal conditions for the duration of their life cycle. Precision farming not only produces higher-quality flowers but also makes it possible to produce flowers all year round, circumventing the constraints imposed by seasonal variations.

There are several benefits to greenhouse farming, from improved environmental control and longer growing seasons to reduced weather-related dangers. The planning and setup of a greenhouse necessitates a thorough understanding of the variables that affect plant development. The effectiveness of controlled environment agriculture, particularly when used with petunias, is demonstrated by how well it creates a customized habitat for the best possible crop development.

CHAPTER SEVEN

HARVESTING AND HANDLING AFTER HARVEST

IDEAL TIME FOR HARVESTING

One crucial component of agricultural operations that has a big impact on crop quality and output is figuring out when to harvest your crops. Harvest time is determined by carefully balancing several variables, including crop maturity, weather, and intended usage. While delaying the harvest may result in overripe food that compromises quality, harvesting too early can lead to undeveloped crops with lesser yields.

For many crops, the best time to harvest coincides with the point of maturity at which the texture, flavor, and nutritional value of the fruits or grains are at their highest. When determining whether crops are ready for harvest, farmers frequently rely on visual clues like firmness and color changes. Furthermore, technical developments like precision agriculture and remote sensing have made instruments for quicker and more precise evaluations available.

TAKING CARE OF AND PACKING

A critical stage in the agricultural supply chain, post-harvest handling entails several procedures used to maintain the quality and increase the shelf life of harvested crops. When produce is handled properly, losses are reduced and its nutritious content is preserved. Sorting, cleaning, and grading are some of the tasks involved in getting rid of broken or unhealthy goods. To prevent physical damage, careful shipping is another aspect of effective handling.

When it comes to keeping harvested commodities' quality intact throughout storage and transit, packaging is essential. Certain crops need different packing materials and methods to avoid bruising, drying out, or rotting.

Packaging also helps to keep an environment under control and shield crops from outside pollutants.

Reducing the environmental impact of post-harvest operations and supporting eco-friendly practices are two reasons why sustainable packaging solutions are becoming more and more important in the agriculture sector.

A crucial step in the post-harvest process is quality control, which makes sure that the harvested products satisfy the requirements needed for both domestic and foreign markets. Measures of quality control cover a range of characteristics, such as size, color, weight, and nutritional value. Technologies like imaging systems and spectroscopy help evaluate the internal and external quality characteristics of crops.

Throughout the post-harvest handling chain, routine testing and inspections are carried out to find and fix any problems as soon as possible. Quality control also includes the production and packaging phases, where it is crucial to follow safety and hygienic guidelines. To keep perishable commodities fresh and prevent spoiling, cold chains must be maintained together with appropriate storage conditions.

The ideas of quality control, handling, packing, and the ideal time for harvesting all play a part in the agricultural supply chain's overall performance. Using best practices in these areas guarantees producers increased yields and financial returns while also providing customers throughout the world with wholesome, safe, and high-quality food.

CHAPTER EIGHT

ADVERTISING TECHNIQUES

BRANDING AND POSITIONING

Branding and positioning are essential elements of any successful marketing plan because they have a significant impact on how the public views a company and its identity. Developing a brand involves more than just coming up with a name or logo; it encompasses the core principles and values of an organization.

It creates a distinctive personality that sets a good or service apart from rivals. Effective branding encourages consumer trust and loyalty to the brand, which affects what they buy.

Conversely, positioning refers to the deliberate and tactical process of establishing a brand's awareness within the intended market. It entails forging a unique identity and connecting the brand to particular characteristics that make it stand out.

A target market that connects with a well-defined brand position is more likely to see the brand favorably and as the top option in its category.

Long-term success in today's dynamic and competitive landscape depends on developing a strong brand and strategic positioning. Delivering brand promises, maintaining a consistent message, and maintaining a visual identity are crucial components of this project.

ONLINE AND OFFLINE MARKETING

As technology has advanced, it has drastically changed the marketing environment and brought about a dynamic interaction between online and offline tactics. The internet and digital platforms have made online marketing essential for reaching a larger and more varied audience.

It includes a range of platforms, including email marketing, social networking, search engine optimization, and online advertising. By utilizing these channels, companies may monitor performance indicators, interact with their target market in real-time, and customize campaigns using insights from data.

Even with the growth of digital marketing, offline tactics are still important, particularly when creating a thorough and coordinated marketing strategy. A well-rounded marketing mix includes conventional techniques like direct mail, events, print advertising, and in-person networking.

An audience connection is strengthened through the physical and personalized touch that offline initiatives frequently offer. A comprehensive brand experience can be produced by combining online and offline channels in a way that maximizes the impact of marketing initiatives.

In the end, a modern marketing plan that is effective acknowledges the mutually beneficial link between offline and online channels and integrates them effectively to increase reach and engagement.

DEVELOPING CONNECTIONS WITH RETAILERS

A key component of marketing strategy is the interaction between merchants and brands, particularly in sectors where goods are distributed through middlemen. For efficient distribution, improved brand awareness, and increased sales, solid relationships with retailers are crucial. Having these kinds of relationships requires open communication, understanding of one another's aims, and working together to accomplish common objectives.

Giving merchants all the product details they need, together with marketing collateral and assistance to help them sell the goods is part of an efficient communication strategy. Brands and retailers should engage in a two-way dialogue to enhance products and maximize marketing tactics.

Co-branding campaigns, cooperative marketing campaigns, and joint promotions can all be effective means of fortifying the relationship between stores and companies. By extending their reach, these initiatives not only help both parties but also build a unified brand image in the eyes of customers.

Successful businesses understand the value of a symbiotic relationship with retailers in today's competitive market, seeing them as strategic partners rather than just distributors. This strategy creates a cooperative atmosphere that benefits both parties and advances the brand's overall performance in the marketplace.

CHAPTER NINE

EVALUATION OF FINANCIAL MANAGEMENT

EXPENSES

One of the most important aspects of financial management is cost estimation, which is estimating the costs related to a specific project, activity, or business operation. Planning and decision-making in the financial domain require accurate cost estimation. It includes determining and estimating a range of costs, including indirect costs like administrative expenditures and direct costs like labor, materials, and overhead.

An effective cost estimation method gives businesses important information about the financial requirements of their projects, empowering them to spend resources wisely and create budgets that fit their needs.

INCOME FORECASTS

Conversely, revenue projections entail projecting the amount of money that a company or project is anticipated to bring in over a given time frame. This procedure aids in setting reasonable financial objectives for firms and is essential to strategic planning. Several variables, including market developments, consumer demand, pricing tactics, and competitive dynamics, are taken into consideration when projecting revenue. Businesses can predict future revenue streams and spot growth possibilities by carefully examining these components. Precise revenue estimates also facilitate efficient budgeting, guarantee long-term financial stability, and help match available resources with projected income.

FINANCIAL PLANNING AND BUDGETING

A blueprint for allocating resources and accomplishing financial goals is provided by budgeting and financial planning, two essential elements of financial management. Budgets are financial plans that show anticipated income and expenses for a given period. They support businesses in setting spending priorities, managing expenses, and gauging success against predetermined standards.

A well-organized budget supports long-term strategic goals in addition to offering a foundation for daily financial operations. Developing strategies to achieve financial objectives while taking risk management, investment planning, and capital structure into account is known as financial planning. Financial planning and budgeting are dynamic procedures that need to be reviewed and adjusted regularly to reflect shifting organizational priorities and the state of the economy.

Budgeting, revenue forecasting, and cost estimate are related ideas that are essential to efficient financial management. While revenue estimates help firms set realistic financial targets, accurate cost estimation serves as the cornerstone of realistic budgeting. These ideas work well together to promote resource allocation, well-informed decision-making, and general financial stability. These ideas, which are dynamic components of financial management, enable businesses to successfully negotiate the challenges of the marketplace and attain long-term financial success.

CHAPTER TEN

LEGAL ASPECTS TO TAKE INTO ACCOUNT

REGULATIONS FOR PETUNIA FARMING

Similar to other agricultural activities, petunia farming is governed by several regulations that are designed to protect the produce, maintain a sustainable environment, and uphold moral standards. These rules, which cover requirements on land usage, water management, pesticide application, and general farming practices, may differ according to the area or nation.

Respecting these rules is essential for consumer safety and health as well as the health and welfare of the environment.

To maintain a reputable and lawful business, petunia farmers need to be aware of and abide by local, national, and international legislation controlling agricultural methods.

PERMITS AND LICENSES

An essential part of the regulatory environment that farmers have to work within is the license and permission requirements for petunia farming. Starting and running a petunia farming business typically requires obtaining the required licenses and permits. Permits for the use of particular agricultural chemicals, water rights, and land use licenses are examples of these papers. The integrity of the agricultural industry as a whole is enhanced when farms adhere to licensing standards, which guarantee that the farm operates within the legally established boundaries set by authorities. Petunia growers must communicate with the appropriate government organizations to comprehend and comply with the permission and licensing requirements unique to their region.

INTELLECTUAL PROPERTY RIGHTS (IPR)

In the petunia industry, IPRs cover the safeguarding of novelties about plant varieties, breeding techniques, and genetic resources. To preserve their discoveries, breeders of novel and distinctive petunia varieties may apply for intellectual property rights, such as plant patents or plant variety rights. Breeders are given the only authority to manage how their created varieties are used, sold, and distributed because of these laws. Petunia farmers need to be aware of and mindful of the intellectual property rights about the particular types of petunias they grow. The legal ramifications of unapproved replication or dissemination of petunia cultivars that are protected may underscore the significance of comprehending and complying with intellectual property regulations in the agriculture domain. Furthermore, upholding a just and moral standard when it comes to intellectual property promotes creativity and the agricultural community's ongoing production of robust and varied petunia cultivars.